THE MAP

A Spiritual Guide to Your Soul's Journey

Amy Antonellis, Kristi Johnston,
Andrea Kukulka

Illustrated by Kristi Johnston

BALBOA.
PRESS

A DIVISION OF HAY HOUSE

Balboa Press books may be ordered through booksellers or by contacting:

Balboa Press
A Division of Hay House
1663 Liberty Drive
Bloomington, IN 47403
www.balboapress.com
1 (877) 407-4847

Print information available on the last page.

ISBN: 978-1-9822-2489-9 (sc)
ISBN: 978-1-9822-2490-5 (e)

Library of Congress Control Number: 2019903689

Balboa Press rev. date: 06/24/2019

Praise for The Map

"*The Map* was enlightening to me in the sense that it provides a visual of the life path I want to take. The steps are simple and make perfect sense. Using our innate intuition as a guide, *The Map* makes it easier to navigate life, whether we are looking to grow as a person or tackle life's challenges, including people we might not mesh with at a given moment. The process gives us more confidence in ourselves. A must read."
Mónica Fernandes, MA, RMT, Author

"*The Map* has been such a wonderful guide for me. It truly is a map of where I am at any given time on this journey of mine. It helps me to understand things and is a constant reference companion for me."
Melanie Sprague, RMT

"*The Map* is a wonderful tool to help guide your journey, provide a compass for direction, and bring clarity and confidence to decision making in building authenticity in life. This is a resource that keeps on giving."
Leigh-Ann Larson, LMHC

"A profound and transformative work designed to enlighten the seeker to discover their soul's purpose."
Rev. Doreen C. Noble, OSF, RMT

Acknowledgements

We would like to thank our families, friends, and our tribe for their support, love, and encouragement on our journey.

Dedication

We dedicate this book to our dads: Mark Driscoll, Clark Dagenkolb, and Jimmy Grevelis.

The Map

Image of *The Map* channeled from Great Spirit by Kristi Johnston, Amy Antonellis and Andrea Kukulka in October 2016.

The description contained herein of what each aspect of *The Map* represents and how to use it as a process to assist you on your life's journey was channeled directly by Kristi, Amy and Andrea in December 2016. Additional content added in February 2017.

Contents

The Map

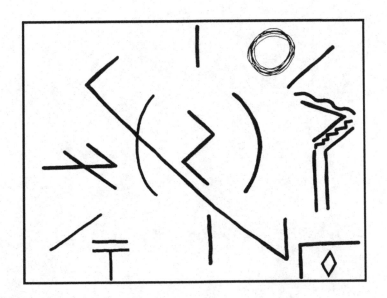

Introduction

Each of these women's journeys began with a simple desire to know more, to understand more, to be more fully connected to Spirit and to themselves. They are three ordinary women with very different backgrounds, in different places in their lives, yet they have become so closely tied to one another that they are aware of each other's physical and emotional states even when they are many miles apart.

They found each other in the spring of 2014 and immediately became friends. After spending much time together laughing, crying and growing, it was clear that they were together for a reason bigger than any of them as individuals and they knew they had work to do. It is also a wonderful truth that it is in fact their individuality and unique perspectives that make their trio greater than the sum of its parts. When they are channeling, they each hear and deliver slightly different versions of the same message. They look at the world through different lenses of experience and have within them differing strengths that complement one another. We point this out to help you notice that it is exactly **your** uniqueness that is important to cherish, to fully allow, and to let shine brightly for the world's benefit.

The words in this book are for you to use to develop a clearer sense of your path and purpose here in this physical plane. You have many questions and even when you have felt that you know who you are and where you are going, you sometimes experience confusion, second-guessing, and self-doubt. *The Map* and its corollary components are meant to assist you with this. It is a tool to use for re-charging, re-orienting yourself to your true focus, and for working through road blocks that keep you from discovering your maximum potential.

Let us begin by describing how *The Map* came to be. One day, Andrea had a vision in her mind's eye of bright curved lines, so bright she couldn't see anything else with her eyes. The intensity was painful. She described these twin arcs to Amy and Kristi, but at that point neither could see them or understand their meaning. Months passed with no further vision. During this time the trio came together to devote their full energy and attention on assisting one of them through a health crisis.

The day after this crisis was successfully resolved, Kristi awoke to a vision of math symbols on a rectangular sheet of paper. They seemed to vibrate as if in motion and yet be perfectly clear at the same time. Later that same day they were drawn together unexpectedly. Kristi spoke about these symbols she had seen and mentioned that she didn't understand their importance.

Kristi is the artist in the trio, so naturally Andrea and Amy encouraged her to draw these symbols. As she began to do this, the image she had seen over 8 hours earlier returned immediately to her mind's eye. While she was drawing, Amy and Andrea could see the finished image in their minds as well and offered additional lines that needed to be added or continued. It was during this time the three realized why Kristi couldn't have drawn these symbols earlier. They recognized that the three of them needed to work together, each with their unique vision, to bring this image through to completion.

Once the drawing was completed, they all could feel the powerful energy coming from the symbols. The energy was so strong it pulled on them like a vortex. Right around the center were the twin arcs that Andrea had seen months earlier! The energy she received had been the Lightening Bolt and its intensity kept her from being able to see with her eyes or have the words to describe the images which now were clearly parentheses.

As they sat with these symbols the information came pouring in. It became clear that *The Map* was three-dimensional and that the symbols had a directionality. They could also see that it was multi-layered and that each layer would expand on prior concepts and explore them to greater depths. They began to discern an order and called it "The Path." They were quickly corrected by Spirit who told them it is called *"The Map."* They asked Spirit what it meant and each began to receive information that they all shared together. It was understood that *The Map* was an important contribution which needed to be distributed and that more information would be forthcoming.

The Map is meant to be a guide as well as an explanation of the processes each human follows while on the physical plane. It is powerful in its own right, but it provides the greatest energy as it is shared and understood. Everyone is on a path of self-discovery. Our role here is to learn and experience the world and deepen our connections to each other. It's all about connection.

This information was transmitted via automatic writing. The bulk of it came through in just a few hours in December 2016. Weeks passed while the trio digested the information, talked about it with one another and a few within their circle. Then, in February 2017, they each felt the imperative to focus more intently on it to receive additional information to bring it to completion.

It brings them great joy to share this with you. They

hold the intention that it will answer some of your deepest questions and offer you guidance wherever you are on your journey.

May you be blessed in your reading and usage of *The Map*.

Start Here

Like everyone, you began in the bottom right-hand corner, in the box. Focused on yourself and comfortable inside the constraints of your human physicality, here you believed that those outside of you knew better than you did. You allowed yourself to be led, to conform, and to be directed along a prescribed road.

It is when you were in this place that you were content to let life happen to you, to see events unfold, and to believe that there was a certain amount of luck or happenstance. It is during this time that some become despairing of ever having or being more, as they are yet unaware to what extent they themselves govern what comes to be in their life.

This is a place some remain for their entire lives before beginning their search for more. At some point in time it is normal to outgrow those limitations and begin asking questions about what lies beyond what is perceived. Once those questions arise, it is like pushing the start button which is represented on *The Map* as the diamond inside the open rectangle. *Start Here* acts as a catalyst to growth and understanding since every answer received presents a new quandary that invites further study and inquiry. Once you have begun to ask questions and have them answered, you will never again be content inside the box of your previous life's restrictions.

Since you have already begun your search to find what else is beyond what you can see of this life, you are already out of the *Start Here* box.

Inside the box is where you will find many of your friends and loved ones. Remember that it is not your job to push them beyond their comfort zone. However, if they are asking questions about your journey or their own, please try to assist them. Offer guidance to them with the lessons you have learned. You may even direct them to those who helped you to get outside of your box.

This information is presented to you in order to assist you in understanding those who have not yet left this place of comfort, safety, and security. Recognize that once you were content there too. Have patience with them, and they will be ready to expand in their own time. Aside from living your life to its fullest and leading by example, there is nothing you can or should do to speed their process.

Connection is a vital part of *The Map*. Connecting to everyone in their various places on *The Map* without judgement is a great part of your journey and theirs.

NOTES

Do This First

Parentheses and Lightning Bolt

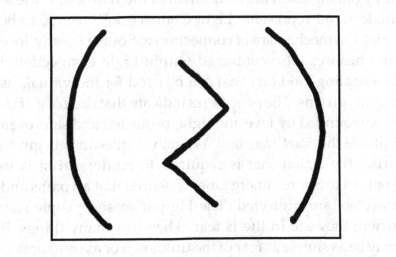

You as the questioner may feel small and vulnerable as you begin to consider the enormity of this universe and the cosmos. You may wonder about your role on this relatively small rock hurtling around a sun. You may not be quite sure where to begin.

We mentioned the intensity of Andrea's initial vision of the parentheses and noted their critical position around the center as well as Kristi's sense that she was seeing math symbols. These are intended to draw your attention here, since in the order of operations in math you perform the action indicated within the parentheses **first**.

The significance of this is that inside the *parentheses* is the *lightning bolt*. This is the symbol the trio have come to understand represents Light Connection™ which, to be brief, is a mechanism of connection to Source Energy, love and healing. Also contained within Light Connection™ is a healing modality that can be used for individuals as well as groups. The *parentheses* indicate that each one of us is surrounded by love and light, protected and safe, even outside the *Start Here* box. Whenever questions begin to arise, the action that is required to be done **first** is to connect to Source Energy. Be reassured that all paths and travelers are protected. The biggest reason people stay where they are in life is fear. They fear many things. It may be as simple as fear of the unknown or as complicated as fear of success. We want to assure you that here, in the arms of the parentheses, you are safe.

At any moment along the journey that you begin to feel uncertain or concerned about your true path, reconnect with Source Energy. It is as easy as placing your hand over the symbol on *The Map*, or imagine that the symbol is already in your hand and place your hand over your heart. Visualize your crown opening to be bathed in the light and love of the Divine. Feel your heart open and notice the connection between that spark of knowing deep inside you and the flow of connection. That is you remembering where you came from and what you are an eternal part of. You are the energy that is everywhere and in everyone.

Whenever life gets hectic or you feel your true self at odds with your circumstances, reach for this reconnection with Source Energy. Better yet, don't wait for things to spin out of control before doing this. Do this **first**.

Reconnect with Source Energy at the beginning of your day, before challenging interactions, as part of your self-care routine.

You are love. You are loved. You deserve to feel this always. All you need to do is reach for it and allow it to permeate your being.

Now read it out loud like this: I am love. I am loved. I deserve to feel this always. There are no strings or conditions. I deserve to feel love always.

NOTES

The Escalator

Now that you have reconnected solidly with Source Energy and remembered that you are safe, the pace really picks up! Like a rocket, you are propelled up *The Escalator* represented by the parallel vertical lines directly above the box.

This stage is one of near constant restlessness. You are searching for truth and ever greater understanding. It is typically a time of extreme focus and discovery, and of modifying your beliefs or even throwing some old beliefs out as you determine them to no longer be relevant. This is a wonderful and exciting time when you should seek out others who are also in this questioning mode and who are open to new ideas and ways of looking at the world and themselves.

It must be noted that this *Escalator* is adjustable in that you may take it as quickly or as slowly as you wish. It is not forced upon you to travel at a prescribed rate that is the same for everyone. This would not make any sense in a world filled with billions upon billions of unique individuals. You absorb and accept each new concept at your own pace and move through the levels of understanding in a way that is perfect for you. It is important that you resist comparing yourself and your progress to others; everyone works at their own comfort level.

Your entire journey is cyclical. You don't work on a concept once and move on, never to think of it again. Instead, you learn one aspect of it, fully integrate it into your life and move on to other topics. When you are ready, you are presented with a deeper understanding of a previous topic and once again are given the opportunity to work through it on this new level before moving on.

This is an especially important time to find a teacher or teachers whose energy resonates with you, who makes you feel empowered, who welcomes your questioning mind, and challenges your status quo. The opportunity to sit with someone who will allow you to express your true desires and deepest "what if" questions while they give you the space to come to your own realizations is priceless.

Do not hesitate to move on from teachers who want you only to think or act a certain way: this is exactly what you are leaving behind. Instead, trust your own knowing and reach inside yourself for the answers and the validation you require. A teacher who presents you with questions so you may seek out your own truth is the right one for you at this stage in your rapid energetic growth.

You will find the right teacher, perhaps in an unexpected place. We are all teachers and we are all students. Find yourself a teacher who continues to learn.

We encourage you to explore teachings from many different sources. Give them all consideration. Check in with your higher self and your intuition and note what feels good and right. You may choose to incorporate those ideas that resonate with you into your new view of All That Is.

Revisit these teachings at different parts of your journey. What seemed outrageous or impossible earlier may now feel completely different. It may fit better (or no longer fit at all) into your new paradigm since you have learned and embraced other concepts once foreign to you.

Each time you arrive at *The Escalator* it signals a time of quick expansion and deeper understanding of yourself and All That Is. There is always more to discover!

NOTES

The Stairs

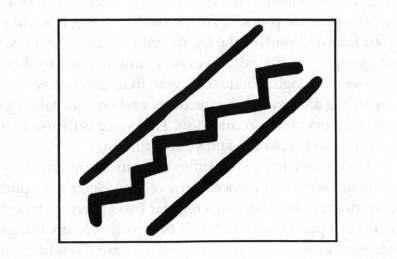

Once you have achieved a certain level of energetic vibration, you reach the diagonal area which is *The Stairs*. This area is not uniform or predictable. It is irregular and uncertain and involves more effort at some points than at others. There is work to be done here.

After the dizzying speed of change during your time in *The Escalator*, it may feel as if you have come to a screeching halt in your development. This is not true. You are **always** expanding and learning. This part does take more work however, so it is necessary to slow down a bit.

Rather than having many ideas presented to you for ingestion, it is instead the time for you to begin searching in earnest inside yourself. This is the time to begin fanning your internal spark of the Divine into a flame. Again we encourage you to find others in a similar stage in their journey. No stage is better or worse than another, each is a learning and growth opportunity and you are called to strive for ever more connection. This stage is focused on your connection to self and your intuition.

Find ways to spend time in your own company without outside influence. Turn off the electronics and disconnect from others on a regular basis, then reconnect with your peers to discuss your discoveries. Many things become clearer when you are able to share thoughts and experiences with others who will understand.

This is a very good time to turn to nature to allow the trees and streams to speak to you. All that you experience at this point is important to your progress through *The Map* and your life's journey. Connect with nature either by being out in it or by bringing its sights, sounds and smells into your space. If you have not already created a sacred space for yourself in your dwelling, it is **essential** that you do so at this time. Surround yourself by those things that resonate with you energetically. Be sure to evaluate each item you place there to ensure it is of the highest possible vibration. Use this space for meditation.

It is inevitable that you will outgrow things. Do not worry, it is normal and right that this is so. Do you still carry a childhood blankie? Do you still wear clothes from your early teen years? Of course not. Once you have moved on physically and emotionally, it is proper for the things you have around you to reflect and support those changes.

Diving into your deepest held beliefs about yourself and the world can be challenging. Find the support system you need for these efforts. Not surprisingly, your family may be the least helpful in these endeavors because they likely hold similar beliefs that you are now ready to leave behind. You are ready to move forward while they would prefer for you to remain who they have known you to be and not upset the family dynamic. Do not hesitate to risk their rejection by broaching the subject of your exploration.

It is quite possible that your friends and family will surprise you with their understanding and tolerance for your growth. Perhaps you will find in them hidden allies who are also moving through this part of their journey but have been keeping it to themselves. You never know until you try.

We do not advise you to hide yourself and your blossoming, but to share where and when appropriate to remain true to yourself. If you do not risk, then you may be depriving yourself and others from welcome understanding and companionship along this new road.

This however is also the time where you must withhold judgement for any who try to hold you back and keep you treading water in the place where you have been, or even push you back towards where you used to be! It is no more their fault for wishing things to stay the same than it is your fault for seeking more understanding and growth. Stand in your full power and glory and surround yourself only with those who support you.

Trust that your intuition will point you in the right direction and affirm connections that will assist you at this time for your continued growth. Be open to meeting new people and taking the time to listen to them with your heart as well as your ears. Lean into the richness of connections made in this way and be guided by how it makes you feel. When you feel that there is give and take and you are resonating with that person and feeling a sense of positivity, you know you have made a good connection.

The Stairs can be a very rewarding phase of your journey. You will get out of it what you are willing to put into it. Be brave. Be brave enough to be totally honest with yourself. Only you can do this for yourself.

The Stairs are only as hard as you make them. Take off the blinders that prevent you from seeing through the illusions of the obstacles you have placed in front of you. See how effortless your path truly is. Spirit never demands that you take the hard route. Make wise choices for yourself. The light will always shine upon you. It is up to you to allow it in and let it guide you.

NOTES

The River

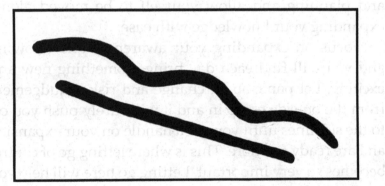

After working through the concepts on *The Stairs* and doing much internal work, you will find the next part of your path smooths out. You have come to *The River*, in other words, the river of life. Here, you may once again choose how quickly you wish to move along in discovery and absorption of new concepts. If you trust and let go of control, you'll find yourself in the swiftly moving center of *The River*.

Perhaps that makes you nervous and so you attempt to steer or drag your feet. If you do so, you will find yourself on *The River's* calmer edges. **You** get to decide. The significance of this is that you will gain awareness in direct proportion to how much you let go of control and planning and allow yourself to be moved along, expanding your knowledge with ease.

Focus on expanding your awareness and allowing and you will find each day brings something new and exciting. Let panic about change and risk or judgement from the outside creep in and it will surely push you off to the sidelines until you get a handle on your expansion and are ready for more. This is where letting go of control becomes so very important. Letting go here will help you to release **all** that holds you back. This is where you learn to **just be**.

Slow or fast, you are always moving forward. No matter how much you fight against it in this stage, you cannot shut off the flow of information coming your way. If you choose to fight against it and swim against the current, it will be exhausting and you may find yourself physically wiped out, in pain, or even ill. Swimming upstream is a product of your own creation. If you are experiencing this, it is time to ask yourself: What is the reason you are trying so hard not to move into the expanded awareness? Why are you resisting your new way of being? Why does it make you uncomfortable? What is it you are really afraid of?

Once you have an answer, you can begin to address the issue head on. It's one thing to think about what is bothering you, but once you put it into words you shift the energy and make it easier to release. A trusted friend is useful for bouncing around ideas and articulating your fears. Perhaps they have dealt with similar issues and can offer insight or at least a compassionate ear. Sometimes a sympathetic ear is all you need to get you moving smoothly again.

The bottom line here is that you hurt no one but yourself by fighting the unknown. You have come far enough along your awakened path to realize there is no turning back, no putting the "genie back in the bottle." So when you're ready, take a deep breath and let go of the need for control. Release the need to know exactly what the future brings. Let go of needing to manage all of the details for how you'll get there and what you'll find when you do.

Manifestation is the act of wanting more and opening up to possibilities. Trust that what you are focused on is waiting for you. Trust that what you have put into motion is about to manifest in your life. You don't *need* to have all the answers about how or when. Expect that it is being handled, even as you read this!

Stop and think for a moment, what were you wishing very hard for a year ago? 6 months ago? 3 months ago? What of those things have come to pass? Take a moment and be grateful for those things and acknowledge your role in bringing them into your life.

What is yet to show up in your life? Do you still want it without reservation? If so, focus your intention and attention on it and see it having already happened. See yourself enjoying what having that in your life feels like and feel grateful for it. Then let go of control and trust that it is on the way.

Relax into the warm, buoyant water and let *The River* carry you right into that life. Let yourself fully experience *The River*: be in the flow of positive, loving energy. Let it flow not only around you, but also through you so that you radiate positive, loving thoughts and actions.

If you allow it, this is the time when you will see the happy effects of your connection with others. You will start to notice that you do indeed have a positive effect on others' lives. This is an opportunity to really **be** the change you wish to see in the world.

Although shining your light for others is of the utmost importance, it is important to remember self-care. Don't forget to keep grounding yourself and attend to your human needs. Do not get so lost in coming to everyone's aid that you forget to be your own best friend and advocate.

Taking care of yourself is not selfish, it is 100% necessary so that you will continue to have the energy to make connections to Source, to yourself and to others. You need to fuel your lamp to keep shining. Do not forget to refill your lamp! Don't wait so long to do so that you allow the flame to be completely extinguished, for it is much harder to restart a lamp that has lost its spark than it is to simply add more fuel to one that is still burning but whose reservoir is low.

We mean to remind you to take time for yourself, to eat well and sleep sufficiently. Spend time in laughter and relaxation and activities that have no other goal than to experience pleasure with people who make you feel good. Live in freedom and authenticity!

Here, we must speak about who you surround yourself with. We mentioned earlier that there may be people in your life who don't wish for you to change. That in and of itself is not a reason to avoid them, but if they begin trying to force you to return to old beliefs or ways of being, then certainly a conversation is in order. You will want to affirm your right to follow your own path while at the same time resisting words of judgement about their choices.

If you feel the relationship is worth it, you may offer the possibility that you agree to disagree on these topics, but they are off-limits. You must take a stand and not tolerate any attempts to change or restrict your journey and expansion. Creating your boundaries and standing by them is very empowering. Allow yourself the opportunity to empower yourself.

You will quickly learn to read those you have this conversation with and know if they are willing to shrug off your differences of opinion or if they are going to dig in their heels and only be happy if you revert to your old ways. You will know in that case that you must significantly limit your time with them, if you decide to continue seeing them at all.

Changing who you spend time with is one very important aspect of changing your energy. Another important aspect is that you will benefit by seeking out those at or above your current vibration. These people are your tribe. You feel positive around them and they are clearly interested in seeing you grow and step into your limitless potential. Surround yourself with these people who think anything is possible, that humans are Divine energy inhabiting physical bodies and that it is important to seek the Divine in everyone. Who you spend time with changes who you are and how you vibrate.

Be quick to lift others up and offer support, but do not be dragged down by those who do not wish to rise. Offer help only if it is asked for, and provide only what they ask for,not what you think they should have. Ego may occasionally step in and you may find yourself enthusiastically trying to pull or push someone forward faster than they are ready or willing to go. You will begin to recognize this and know when it's time to allow the other person more room to proceed on their own journey.

Find your tribe and spend as much time with them as you want. Stop making excuses for why you can't do this. You owe these friendships to yourself. Tribes don't judge, they love. Only allow yourself to be loved. This is essential to your soul.

NOTES

The Interpreter Line and
The Vibrating Circle

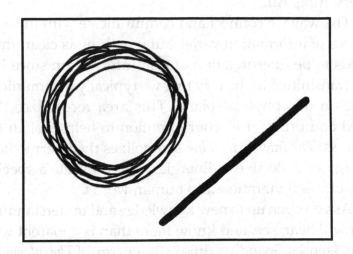

Now we have come to the area of *The Interpreter Line* and *The Vibrating Circle*. The *Circle* represents the Infinite Source of Knowledge, it is All That Is, Was and Will Be. It has multiple lines to show that it is indeed vibrating with boundless energy. Those multiple lines also represent that it is not a flat disc, but instead a multi-dimensional, time-space vortex. This symbol represents all non-physical energy including Spirit Guides, Angels, Archangels, Collectives of Light Beings, Ascended Masters and Saints, Lords of the Akashic Records, and the essences of all those who have been human as well as those who have manifested on physical planes other than earth. Everything. All.

The way we connect and communicate with this vast source of information varies but one thing is clear: there needs to be interpretation of that information since it is not transmitted in the way that we typically communicate here on this physical plane. This area recognizes that need and brings it to your attention to help explain the process. *The Interpreter Line* symbolizes the intermediary Energy or collective of Energies who translate a specific non-physical vibration into human words.

As you open up to new knowledge and understanding, you will hear, see, and know more than is apparent with your 5 senses. Spending time in the energy of *The Interpreter Line* deepens your understanding of the non-physical by providing you with an Interpreter or Interpreters who will facilitate your understanding of All That Is.

This Interpreter may be subtle and even virtually undetectable, working in the background like an air-traffic controller, or they may clearly identify themselves to you. As you gain facility working with the higher vibrational energies you may need less assistance. With each new level you are able to access, you require and will be provided with a new Interpreter to aid in your understanding. As you practice accessing the various levels of information, you will recognize the different energy signatures of each of your Interpreters. Each new frequency provides you with a deeper understanding of All That Is.

Connecting to and being aware of receiving information from energy that is not physical happens to everyone to some degree, but it takes many forms. It may be as you expand your vibration you are more tuned in to the natural world of plant life, animals, water, rocks, weather, or food; or perhaps you will have an increased sense of other people's emotions or physical issues, etc. There are many ways in which you may receive information from non-physical energy. All of these sources of information lie within *The Vibrating Circle* and at least initially will need to be accessed and translated by an Interpreter.

There are many, many methods of expanding your awareness and they all are important! A crucial aspect of increasing your understanding of the world and yourself is to find what draws your attention and lights your fire. Where does your passion lie? What do you wish to know more about? What would give you pleasure to spend time doing every day? Set yourself free to do just that!

We are asking you to tune in to what is most important to you. Please know that it doesn't have to be a huge "end global warming, create world peace" sort of endeavor. The crucial aspect is that it is authentically **your** interest and it brings you joy. Don't underestimate how important what your interests are to those around you. This may be part of your true purpose.

Connecting to yourself in this way allows you to also be connected, often via an Interpreter, to those etheric resources of support and guidance. You have unlimited access, but they can best help you when you ask and *then are open to receiving* their assistance and information.

Finding and owning your true purpose means embracing all of the experiences of living on this physical plane with all of its ups and downs. It means not allowing yourself to get stuck in despair due to challenges, but instead expecting and anticipating that everything will work out for your highest and best.

Pursuing your true purpose means, most importantly, not giving up just because you have not yet achieved your goal. Trust that all you want, need, hope for, and most desire is on its way. You have put the energy out there with your request and now all you have to do is continue to move towards it, one logical step at a time.

NOTES

NOTES

As Above, So Below

As Above, So Below: You may only expand up and out to the same degree that you recognize and support your connection to the physical plane.

Here is a time for contemplation and focus on finding balance in your life. The vertical line in the center of the top and bottom of *The Map* are a reminder that *As Above, So Below*. This is the time for reflection and honesty about your personal efforts and how they affect those around you. Looking outside as well as inside is just as important as connecting to Source and grounding.

Think of a tree. It must send roots down into the ground for support and for nourishment in the same way that it grows up and out, to draw in the light and air for a different kind of sustenance. The strongest trees are those whose roots are as deep and wide as the tree: *As Above, So Below*. Similar to the tree, every person must remain connected to both earth and Spirit.

You are a spiritual being occupying a human body and that must always be taken into consideration. You must honor the human part of yourself at all times. Don't get lost by working so hard on *The Vibrating Circle* that you forget to remain in the now and in your human body. You must go deep down into the earth to ground, to be fully human, and to reach the highest level of connection. Honor your human first and stay in your body in order to soar high. Do not be so concerned about what you are doing that you neglect other important areas or people in your life. Remember to begin by grounding to the earth and connecting to Source.

It is intoxicating to be in Source Energy, safely buffered from whatever is transpiring on your human plane. This is not a state of being that can be safely maintained. It is not the way to fully experience life. Living in your human body with all of its inherent limitations and benefits is what you chose. When you consistently use your connection to Spirit for escape and avoidance, you cheat yourself and your loved ones of your fully engaged presence. You must be completely present in the here and now in order to feel with all of your being what you most desire. Only when you are able to remain grounded and feel your desire with your whole self, will it begin to move towards you.

Balance is required in all things: time for work and play, time for inner contemplation and outward focus, time to learn and time to integrate that learning so it may serve its highest purpose, time to spend in Spirit and time to fully engage in life. Information that hasn't been fully absorbed and understood is gibberish. You must take time to allow each new piece to sink into your consciousness. This means that you must allow time to pass between taking in new information, and in that interim turn your focus towards other aspects of life while you let it sink in.

This process cannot be rushed. It will take however long it takes and it doesn't happen overnight, by pushing it down, or by ignoring it. Be mindful, be deliberate in your desire to bring this unfolding to blossoming. Be patient with yourself.

NOTES

Infinity

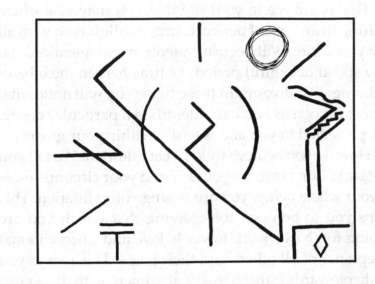

You notice the top left corner of *The Map* is empty. It is empty and it is full. This is the space of *Infinity*, of limitless possibilities that defy description because to describe them is to limit them. This is where all of your dreams, your hopes, and wishes live and can be realized with thought and focus.

This is where your vibration must match the vibration of that which you wish to see manifest in your reality. It is where the knowledge you have uncovered and absorbed allows you to reach for the biggest, most glorious opportunities with unabashed freedom.

This is a place in your life that you may visit often, drifting in and out of perfect energetic alignment with all that you desire. With focused attention and intention, you may spend delightful periods of time here in the bliss of realizing your dreams. In these times you will notice that almost as soon as you have identified a particular desire, it is presented to you and is easily within your grasp.

How do you achieve this? Great question! We tell you that by holding love for yourself and your circumstances in your whole being, you are raising your vibration. This helps you to be open to receiving that which you are hoping for. Next, work towards love and unconditional acceptance of all others and their paths. This moves you further towards pure energetic alignment with the Source Energy of love where all knowledge and abundance reside. See yourself as an observer with only love radiating from you. Practice this whenever judgement of yourself or others sneaks into your heart.

This sounds simple enough, doesn't it? Indeed, it is not complicated, however on your human plane there are many distractions both internal and external that pull you away from this blissful state of perfect alignment with Divine love.

Do not berate yourself for not maintaining this state always. This is exactly why we told you that it would be a place you would visit. Relish those times when you **are** in perfect alignment. Notice even the shift from your 'typical' to **improved** alignment where life flows more easily and pleasantly. The more you notice this, the easier it will be to reach for this feeling and magnify it. Reaching for a better vibration will become a habit and you will be able to do it even when the road of life gets a little bumpy.

When you think of *Infinity* we know that it is a concept so enormous that you can't wrap your mind around it fully. Nonetheless we ask you to be open to the potential that is there. You really can have everything you wish for without limits. The limits you imagine are fully self-imposed. There is rarely a need for either this **or** that, but instead there is room for this **and** that.

Do not let your fear of change stop you here. Your ego will attempt to squash your most extravagant hopes by telling you things like: You can't, you don't deserve it, who do you think you are, you might fail, or what will people think. These are all normal and it is your ego's job to try to keep you small and comfortable in familiar surroundings with predictable outcomes.

It is your job to tell ego to take a back seat and let you drive the car into the unknown with complete confidence that at the end of the ride you will land exactly where you want to be. This must be done while acknowledging that fear will ride with you. Feeling fearful is how you know you are about to do something important for your growth.

Here, you are encouraged to fail. It's ok to fail. In fact, it's great to fail because you learned what doesn't work. Now you have more information and are closer to being successful. Keep trying until you have accomplished what you set out to achieve. You are a limitless being with infinite potential. Keep going!

Failure is merely a bump in the road, you are much greater than the sum of your failures. Pick yourself up by the bootstraps and keep going! The world is yours for the taking.

NOTES

Abundance

Now you have arrived at the *Abundance* symbol. This is the limitless manifestation of all you need in life. Money, health, love, connection, travel, learning, etc. You name it, you can choose to have it and have it in **abundance.** This is not just the universe meeting your basic needs, it is you purposely *drawing towards you* exactly what you want in any quantity you desire. **Most importantly, it doesn't have to be hard.**

It is not required that you spend years toiling away, handling one difficulty after another to finally get what you want. Struggle is not automatically part of the *Abundance* equation. You can enjoy the money and freedom to travel, find love and true connection, live in wellness and wonder; all without back-breaking, spirit-quelling work.

Abundance represents **more than enough.** Take a moment and allow this to settle in. **More than enough.** If you are in this place in your life, you are aware that there really is no need to worry about enough money to pay the bills, enough food for yourself or your family, enough hours in the day. You understand that your needs are met if you stay out of your own way and say yes to opportunities that arise, whether you think yourself qualified or not. You must understand fully and completely that it takes just as much energy to have enough as it does to have more than enough. **That's right, you can have more!**

The stumbling block we hear you placing in front of you is fear of greed. Are you greedy to want more than you need? Is it selfish to want more for yourself when others have even less than you currently have?

The answer is layered. Wanting more is part of recognizing that you can **have** more. Just because you have more does not mean you're taking from others, they can choose to have more as well! Being fully supported in abundance includes being willing to accept such support and embracing all of the joys that the world has to offer.

Now, what will you do with more than you need once you have it? When you have arrived at this place on your journey, we think you can easily answer with conviction that you will use the extra resources to continue to grow, expand, and share the resulting increase, whatever that may be.

You already do that, don't you? When you learn something new, don't you delight in sharing it? When you develop a new skill that can help someone else you use it, correct? When you find yourself with plenty of money don't you do something nice with it? We are confident that those whose prime objective is amassing enormous amounts of money without doing anything positive in the world are on a different path than those who are reading this. Make no bones about it, the Universe wants you to have this abundance so that you may do good with it, so that you can help those who need it, **and** for your own enjoyment.

If you are worried about greed, it is unlikely that you are greedy. Quiet your fear and write down the top 3 causes you would support with your extra money. Recognize that there is one cause that speaks to you more loudly than all the rest. Think about how it would feel to support that cause financially in a truly meaningful way? Can you picture yourself writing a check with many zeros? See yourself handing it to the person in charge and designating how you would like it used? Now that's a feeling, isn't it?! Go ahead, contemplate abundance and reach for it without hesitation or shame. Do it now!

Of all the things that you may wish for an abundance of, health is perhaps the most challenging. Maintaining your health is within your control, however it is easy to lose focus.

Lack of health is your body's way of getting your attention and asking you to focus your energy in a different direction. It is even occasionally Spirit's method of forcing you into much-needed but previously resisted, down time.

However, some health issues are like a large rock rolling downhill. Once certain processes are set in motion, they become nearly impossible to halt or reverse. Many of these may have been initiated long before you had awareness of the mind-body connection. We caution you to avoid blaming yourself for not avoiding these difficulties or for not being able to reverse them. Instead, we ask you to find the opportunities for growth and learning within these challenging times.

In the midst of pain, disease or infirmity, can you still find your inner peace, comfort, and connection to Source love? Aim for acceptance of what cannot be changed. Seek help from any source that feels right to you and welcome and allow whatever relief or assistance they can provide. Being unwell is **never** a punishment to be endured stoically without aid. You are entitled to feel and be as healthy and comfortable as is possible, under any circumstances.

Now that you have begun to feel what abundance means to you, you must be willing to receive it. This is a different step and it is one of allowing. It is necessary for you to work through any residual blocks or walls that would prevent you from gracefully accepting all the Universe wants to send your way. Stop rejecting Universal gifts, even when doing so subconsciously. Consider how many times you have rejected someone's warm gesture for fear of being greedy or an inconvenience. Spend time doing a bit more internal evaluation to see if you can find and release what may be deeply buried and causing you to make such rejections. You cannot achieve abundance if you cannot receive it.

There are as many ways of finding and releasing emotional blocks or walls as there are reasons you built them. There is no singular way that works for everyone. Light Connection ™ is one of the ways you may use to experience a big release in a relatively short period of time. Energy and body work of various forms will assist you in this process.

Be aware that you may have placed many layers of resistance to finding true personal acceptance and love. While these restraints are present, they will limit your ability to receive abundance. Don't be dismayed if you work through one layer and later find another. You are a complicated and marvelous human. Don't give up the promise of experiencing **all** you long for. It's worth the effort!

Be tender with yourself at this time and tread gently on old wounds as you uncover them. These wounds will heal with your acceptance of how they came to be. Forgiveness is the key. Open your heart to forgive yourself. Embrace your past: it is essential to your make-up. Old issues need to be released, but do not chastise yourself for their existence.

If you are still feeling stuck and you have done your best to detect the cause unsuccessfully, it's time to contact someone you have confidence in and who understands these types of challenges. There may be something from a past life that a past life regression or a session with your Akashic Records could shed some light to help you resolve it. It may be that you need guidance on inner child work or releasing cords or attachments. Talk to a reputable holistic healer and they should be able to point you in the right direction on how to approach and dissolve these blocks.

Much of this work can be done virtually so do not let the time or expense of travel limit who you seek out for assistance. You must resonate with that person in order to have complete trust. Feel their energy. Does it match your own? We are all made of energy. Your healer's energy should never overpower yours, it should complement and bring to light that which is within you. These are private areas of your essence and as such deserve the utmost respect and compassion from whomever you choose.

When you are ready to fully embrace *Abundance*, you are ready to revisit the question of what brings you the most joy. What would you do every day for free if you had no need for money? This is your opportunity to consider the possibility that you could make a very good living doing what you truly love and are uniquely suited to do. Do not continue doing what you think you "should" because someone told you to, it's what you studied, or it's all you've ever done.

What makes you excited to get up in the morning? What keeps you up late at night because it's just so interesting you can't stop? We are not suggesting that you quit your day job to begin trekking across the continent just because you've always loved hiking. We are instead asking you to find ways each day to incorporate more of what you love and to begin seeing how that time could be expanded. There may be a time in the nearer future than you expect when you are able to shift what you do for income to only things you love most.

One step at a time is the way to get there. Keep envisioning what a life lived in that way looks and feels like. Then take that next step in confidence that another will be laid out in front of you as soon as you are ready for it.

NOTES

Interpreter Line and Antenna

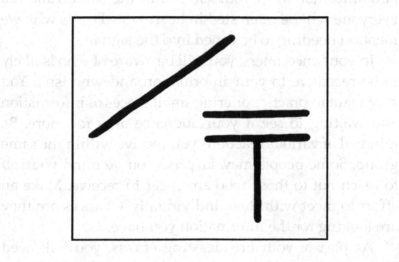

We have arrived at another *Interpreter Line* and it is related to the *Antenna* directly underneath it. The first *Interpreter Line* was about you receiving information from higher energetic vibrations and needing to have the non-physical communication translated for your understanding. Now, you need to become the interpreter to share all that you have discovered to be true with others. This sharing is represented by the *Antenna*.

An antenna broadcasts a signal and those who are tuned into the signal may receive whatever is being broadcast. You have a responsibility to avoid keeping this new information to yourself, but at the same time not everyone will be interested in hearing it. This is why we mention needing to be tuned into the signal.

In your encounters, you will be aware of who is likely to be receptive to your information and who isn't. You may want to practice offering small pieces of information and waiting to see if your audience asks for more. Be mindful of various reactions you receive within the same group. Some people may surprise you. Remind yourself to reach out to those who are eager to receive. Make an effort to meet with them individually. Chances are they are looking for the information you have.

As part of your broadcasting efforts, you will need to be a beacon of light, love and compassion. This way, others who are searching and ready for the information will find you. This also makes it easier to determine who to share the information with.

Becoming the interpreter is another way that you make the information yours and let it fully sink into your being. By translating what you have learned into your own words, you expand your depth of knowledge.

When you share it with others, you are facilitating their comprehension by having filtered it through your own experience.

As you act as an interpreter for others, you will find that your understanding of each aspect of *The Map* increases. You will also notice that life is flowing more easily for you, you are staying grounded more easily, and you are connected to Source and yourself more fully. You will also find that you manifest more easily and feel more confident.

It is like anything new: there is a learning curve and time is required to practice and gain mastery of each aspect of this new skill. The efforts you exert enhance your abilities and eventually you don't need to think about each part, they happen automatically and without conscious intention. Be gentle with yourself during this time of discovery.

NOTES

The Shortcut

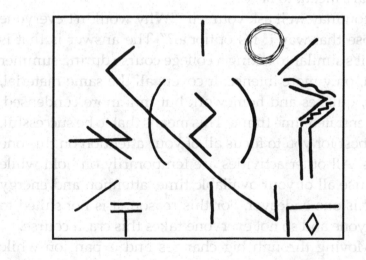

The last aspect of *The Map* is the diagonal line through the center bracketed by shorter lines. This is *The Shortcut*. Much like in the childhood game *Chutes and Ladders*, this section represents an opportunity to quickly bypass a large area all at once. Like a seesaw, it is balanced but moveable. Its pivot point is the *Lightning Bolt*, the anchoring connection to Source. Thanks to its three-dimensional characteristic, it is free to rotate and tip between any two places on *The Map*. So you see, it doesn't matter where you are or where you are determined to go when you choose *The Shortcut*. Rest assured you will end up exactly where you are meant to be.

You may well ask yourself: "Why wouldn't everyone choose that way if it's optional?" The answer is that is that it's similar to taking a college course during summer term, only more intense. It covers all the same material, tests, quizzes and homework but in a more condensed, concentrated time frame. This means that to be successful, it is best for you to focus all of your attention on this one class. All other activities are temporarily on hold while you use all of your available time, attention and energy on this one endeavor. For this reason, it is not suited to everyone and so not everyone takes this crash course.

Moving through big changes and expansion while simultaneously finding and releasing what no longer serves you, and processing it all in this condensed manner is challenging. Using the shortcut is always a choice.

If you choose *The Shortcut* to conquer a particular aspect of learning, know that you will essentially be consumed with that effort for the duration of the process no matter how long it takes.

If you are very impatient, you may notice in retrospect

that you have manifested yourself on a shortcut more than once as you have railed against the time it takes to make noticeable progress in certain areas of your life. If, at any time, you recognize that you have landed on a *Shortcut* and wish to change course and return to the typical path, you need only to practice patience with yourself and your journey. See yourself taking more time for this learning and seek balance with other aspects of your life. Similarly, if you are on the typical path and wish to accelerate your growth, hold the intention that you will take *The Shortcut* and blast through everything necessary to arrive on the other side.

A consideration before launching yourself along this track is to arrange for the required support for as long as this may take, both in practical matters of daily life and emotional and spiritual support. The intensity of *The Shortcut* may feel overwhelming to you. Know and respect your needs.

This is another time to carefully consider who will be there for you. Be certain they are dependable and have your best interests at heart, for you will be quite vulnerable during this massive expenditure of energy and effort.

The benefit of *The Shortcut* is primarily in the physical time saved. You will see huge progress in your ability to let go, trust, allow, receive, and love in a few months or less compared to years. Your connection to Source Energy and your self-awareness will also expand enormously. Yes, there is a price you will pay and it comes in the form of extreme physical and emotional challenges. It requires that you focus all of your time, energy, and attention on remaining grounded throughout the process.

Your patience and stamina will be tested. You will be forced to ask for and accept assistance, and in the process learn how to do so with grace. The lessons you learn in each *Shortcut* you choose will be yours forever. Once the lessons are learned you may quickly turn your attention to the next important part of your journey. Being aware of both the challenges and the benefits will help you decide when and if to use *The Shortcut*.

NOTES

About Time

We also wish to speak about the directionality of *The Map*. You may have noticed that it sends you in a counter-clockwise manner. This is quite purposeful for we wish to interrupt your focus on time as linear and clockwise, measured and divided into perpetually equal segments.

Now that you have gotten this far you need to open your perception to the myriad ways that time is fluid and variable.

You have had occasions where it seemed as if you accomplished far more in the allotted time that you thought was possible. You have had situations that passed far more quickly than your awareness detected. This is not because you were busy, for there are instances when being busy may result in time passing more slowly or those where it moves more quickly. What matters is not the type or level of activity, your awareness or lack thereof, it is instead what would most serve you and what your intention is regarding the passage of time. We are saying that you can control time to a certain extent. Time is fluid.

Another way to think of it is to say that you control your movement within time. Similarly to how you can control your speed as you move through a river by altering the placement of your body, you may do this with the flow of time as well. You may choose to allow it to pass in its culturally accepted fashion or you may play with its variability to suit your circumstances.

Having a fabulous time on vacation? Stretch time out and alter your perception so it seems as if it's two weeks instead of one. Running behind on your morning commute? Focus on arriving in the parking lot at the perfect time to allow your entrance right on schedule. Impatient to finish your day? Move things along and see yourself out the door sooner rather than later. Make time work for you!

This is not a directive to wish your life away or a remedy for perpetual tardiness, but instead an invitation to consider allowing time to work with and for you instead of seeing it as the enemy. You may argue that time affects other people and playing with it may create issues beyond your scope of understanding. This is true to a point, but since we are really talking about how you personally move through time versus changing the speed with which time passes for everyone, it has fewer complications.

It is harder to modify experiences that are shared with another person or persons unless they too are in the habit of manipulating time to their advantage. If they are, then your efforts are magnified and it becomes easier to achieve the same outcome. This is yet another reason to surround yourself with like-minded people: a pleasant experience that you are all enjoying and collectively choose to extend will seem to magically go on for ages!

NOTES

Conclusion

Looking at *The Map* you may think you are done. This is far from the truth. As we mentioned earlier, the path is similar to a spiral that keeps circling back. Each time you revisit a concept, you are able to find out more details and gain a deeper understanding, to work through more of your old belief systems and release restrictions.

This is not a journey that correlates with your years on earth. At any point in your life you may be at any place on *The Map*. Use *The Map* for reassurance and as your personal guide and a point of reference. It is useful to see where you are, where you have been, where you are going, and to offer guidance when requested by others along the path. It is a tool to use as a starting point for making meaningful connections. As you identify which stage you are in and speak about your journey, you will find common ground with others. It is from this place where mutual understanding and respect are born.

Do not compare your journey to anyone else's. Do not judge yourself as you see someone else ahead of you on *The Map*. You have no idea how many times they have been around *The Map* already, nor do you have an understanding of how many rotations you have completed. *The Map* is in constant motion. The motion contained within *The Map* is a reflection of your continuous journey. At no point does it start or end. Be assured that once you have left the starting box, you need not ever return. Do not place restrictions on how many times you can take this journey. It is not important to note how many or few times you make the rotation, the purpose is to enjoy the ride. There are too few of you who even bother to do so. We ask you to enjoy your journey at this time.

NOTES

Now What?

69

This completes the information for the first layer of *The Map* and what each area represents regarding your journey of learning, discovery and expansion. There are more layers and each section has expanded views which will be described at another time. For now, this is sufficient for you to contemplate and sit with.

Once you have read through this book, do it again. You will be surprised what is revealed during a second reading. You may wonder what to **do** with this information. Here are some suggestions:

1. Place your hand above or on the symbols one at a time. Feel the energy from the symbols. Notice which you resonate with most at this time.
2. Choose the symbol you are most drawn to as a beginning place for meditation and/or automatic writing to open to a deeper meaning for you personally at this time.
3. Discuss the information with peers and use it as a point of connection and understanding as you share your journey with others.
4. When having energy work done, focus on the area you are headed to next and allow yourself to receive what you need, to move into it with comfort and grace.

Rest assured, you are fully supported at every stage along your path, you need only to be open to how that support shows up and be willing to receive it.

Blessings to you and your understanding of these words.

NOTES

About the Authors

The Center for Holistic Healing and Art is comprised of Amy Antonellis, Andrea Kukulka, and Kristi Johnston. They are all Reiki Master Teachers and have been working together weekly since spring of 2014, channeling messages from Angels, Archangels, Guides, and various collectives of Light Beings. They perform healing energy work together and separately in their community and surrounding areas, as well as present their channeling of loved ones in spirit for individuals and groups.

Recently they have been called to broaden their reach

by presenting in public not only messages from passed loved ones, but also messages from the collective of Light Beings they know as Great Spirit. Great Spirit is the group who transmitted a new form of energy healing called Light Connection™ to Amy, Andrea and Kristi in March of 2015. Great Spirit has continued to work with them regularly and has become a large part of everything they do involving energy work.

Andrea has been active in the metaphysical world since the late 1980's, studying many forms of energy healing and using her intuitive gifts as well as bringing healing messages from passed loved ones. She now does this work full time and is highly sought after for her amazing gifts as an energy healer, Reiki Master Teacher, and as a medium.

Amy is a practicing attorney and has been expanding her intuitive and channeling talents since 2013. She is dedicated to assisting people in times of transition and as a founding partner in a law firm and holistic center, she is able to offer practical as well as emotional support to all of her clients.

Kristi is an artist, art instructor, and energy healer. She was a Physical Therapy Assistant for 30 years. Having discovered her intuitive gifts in early 2014, she is the newest to join the metaphysical party. Her strongest gifts lie in emotional connection, reading the Akashic Records, and spirit art.

When these three very different women come together to join their unique energies and perspectives, they always bring you a very powerful and energy-expanding experience. Their main goal is always to share love and connection, whether it be through channeling messages or bringing you direct healing.

Printed in the United States
By Bookmasters

Printed in the United States
By Bookmasters